Magnificent
COLORADO

Photography by
Todd Caudle

Colorado
Souvenir
Series

Skyline Press
Pueblo, Colorado

Magnificent
COLORADO

Photography by
Todd Caudle

Published by Skyline Press
311 West Evans Avenue
Pueblo, Colorado 81004
ISBN: 1-888845-06-6
Printed in Hong Kong

Front Cover: Maroon Bells reflected in Maroon Lake
Back Cover (left to right): Ice Mountain, Collegiate Peaks;
Fall colors, Cimarron Range; Mount Guyot reflection
Title Page: Sunset over the distant Gore Range
from the slopes of Tiptop Peak

Colorado blue columbines, Gunnison National Forest

Aspen canopy, White River National Forest

Introduction

Another spectacular July day in Colorado. The weather was clear. The sky was as blue as I'd ever seen it. And the winter snowpack, by now all but a memory, had nourished the landscape and turned it a rich, summery green. Wildflowers proliferated on the open tundra, making the hike up Elliott Ridge all the more enjoyable. For five miles I traveled up this open expanse in the Eagles Nest Wilderness in northern Colorado, making my way toward a trail junction that would lead me to the headwaters of Cataract Creek. And for this opening segment of the trip I was continually rewarded with distant views of Colorado's diverse landscape. To the north were the craggy, glacially-carved peaks of Rocky Mountain National Park. To the southwest, the Elk Mountains sat on the horizon like giant thrones — still visible a month into summer was the massive snowfield that gave Snowmass Mountain its name. Closer at hand, just across the valley that cradles Green Mountain Reservoir, the Williams Fork Mountains, where I had spent the previous night, turned blue as the haze of afternoon set in. But the best view of all was directly south, towards my destination. Though Colorado justifies almost any superlative one would care to utter, the Gore Range that I was now hiking in stands as some of its most beautiful real estate. Ahead of me, Mount Powell, Eagles Nest, Meridian Peak and a host of unnamed summits beckoned. Their beauty made my pack feel just a little bit lighter.

When I finally made it to the Cataract Creek trail junction, I paused. Rather than immediately trade my uphill battle for an easier downhill jaunt, I sat in a grassy meadow, surveying the landscape before me. A small stream burbled across the tundra nearby, fed by one of the few remaining snowfields from winter storms past. Overhead, afternoon clouds drifted effortlessly across a deep blue sky. And I thanked my lucky stars that this is the life I chose.

Throughout this book there are many stories like the one above, if only in my mind's notebook. Almost every photograph I make has a special memory attached to it. Maybe a sunrise unlike any I had ever seen, or a winter snowstorm that left a fairyland of white in its wake. Maybe there was a year when the aspens didn't turn as brilliantly gold as they normally do, but I was lucky enough to find that perfect grove shimmering in the autumn sun. That's what makes being a landscape photographer so special. As I travel around our great country, I am constantly reminded that the place that I call home is, in all honesty, America's jewel in the crown. Little wonder that it is a land that inspired the writing of "America the Beautiful." Colorado is that and so much more.

— Todd Caudle

Eagles Nest reflection, Eagles Nest Wilderness

Garden of the Gods
Kissing Camels • Cathedral Rock reflection

A light dusting of powder on Pikes Peak
Overleaf: Aspens below Cottonwood Pass, San Isabel National Forest

Black Canyon of the Gunnison National Park
North Rim • Painted Wall
Sunset View • Gunnison River

Sunrise at Painted Wall overlook

Moonset over Music Mountain, Sand Creek Lakes, Sangre de Cristo Wilderness

Full moon and Earth's shadow, Sharkstooth Peak, La Plata Mountains

Marsh marigolds in the Missouri Lakes Basin, Holy Cross Wilderness

Headwaters of Cross Creek, Holy Cross Wilderness

Fresh snow in the Wet Mountains

Clearing storm over Mount Arkansas, Mosquito Range

Aspen gold below Marcellina Mountain, Gunnison National Forest

Autumn comes to the Cimarrons, below Owl Creek Pass

Foggy morning, North Clear Creek Falls, Rio Grande National Forest

Waterfall detail, San Juan Mountains

Overleaf: Winter wonderland at sunset, Tenmile Range

A broad pallette of fall color below Marcellina Mountain, Kebler Pass Road

Autumn aspens of the Sierra Blanca, Sangre de Cristo Mountains

Rainbow over abandoned cabin, Rio Grande National Forest

Star Mine sunrise, Italian Mountain

Mountain goats, Grays Peak

Rocky Mountain bighorn sheep, Mount Evans

Hallett Peak in winter

Moonset over the Never Summer Mountains

Sunset over the Mummy Range

Rocky Mountain National Park

Longs Peak from the Rock Cut

Overleaf: Elk scars on aspen trees, along the Bear Lake Road

White landscape, Never Summer Mountains, Rocky Mountain National Park

Wilson Peak in winter, San Miguel Mountains

Autumn reflection, Sangre de Cristo Range

Forest road, La Plata Mountains

Orange sneezeweed, Elk Mountains

Lupine, Gore Range

Wildflower garden on Stony Pass, Rio Grande National Forest

Great Sand Dunes

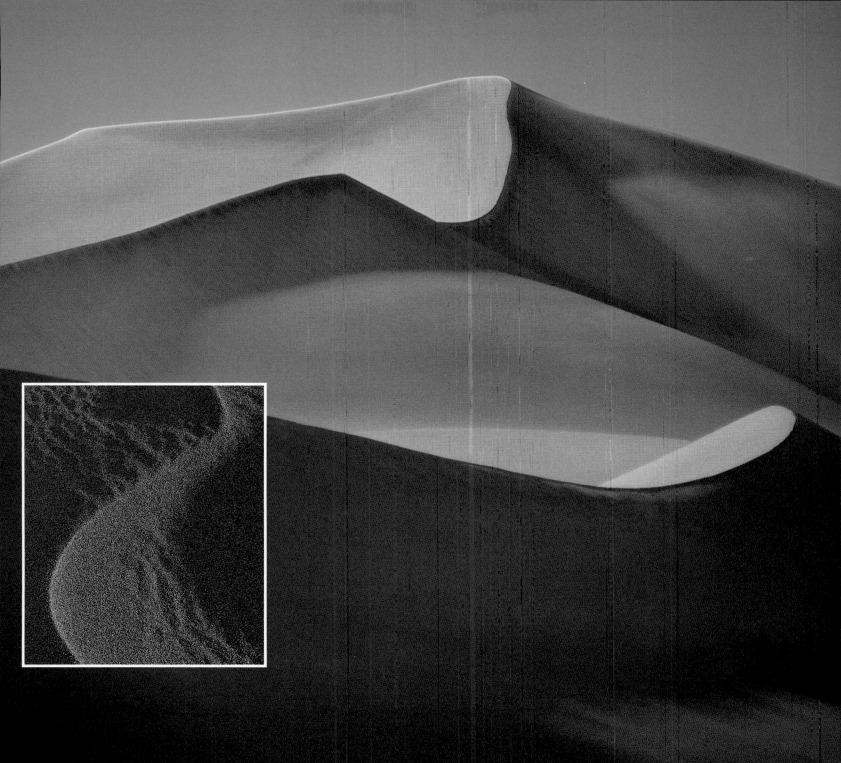

Waterfall below Stony Mountain, Yankee Boy Basin, San Juan Mountains

Red Mountain No. 1 reflection, San Juan Mountains

The season's first snow, along Maroon Creek, White River National Forest

Autumn gold below McClure Pass

Last winter's snow meets this summer's flow below Mount Toll, Indian Peaks Wilderness

Above the clouds, the Three Apostles, Collegiate Peaks Wilderness

Heartleaf arnica along Paradise Road, Gunnison National Forest

Ironworks and Mount Crested Butte

Sandstone formations in Monument Canyon, Colorado National Monument

Sunset on Pyramid Peak, Maroon Bells-Snowmass Wilderness

Maroon Bells and Fravert Basin, Maroon Bells-Snowmass Wilderness

Summer meadow in the Sawatch Range, San Isabel National Forest

Overleaf: Spectacular sunset over Rio Grande Reservoir, San Juan Mountains